WE ALL THINK DIFFERENTLY

BY H.J.RAY

MY NEURODIVERSITY GUIDEBOOK

WE ALL THINK DIFFERENTLY

This workbook is for children 8+ and their parents, carers, teachers, or therapists to inspire open-ended dialogue about what it means to be smart, how intelligence looks different to everyone and build empathy and understanding for some of the challenges neurodivergent people face and the strengths that come from these different perspectives.

For more helpful resources on neurodiversity and wellbeing education, visit www.mywellbeingschool.com

Text and illustrations Copyright 2023. Published by My Wellbeing School.

Celebrate Neurodiversity

Accept
WE ALL THINK DIFFERENTLY.

Understand
OTHER POINTS OF VIEW EXIST.

Respect
WE ARE ALL SMART IN OUR OWN WAY.

Embrace
YOUR UNIQUE MIND.

NOTE FROM THE AUTHOR:

I didn't struggle at school. I was lucky. Not that I was very good at Maths or English, or because I was particularly well-behaved in class; in fact, I was likened to Marmite (or the much less delicious Aussie variation - Vegemite.) I was an acquired taste. I do remember my middle school maths teacher calling me an alien in front of the class and saying that I must be from another planet because I couldn't grasp the concepts he was teaching... he clearly wasn't a Marmite fan.

But, one teacher changed the way I thought about my intelligence, and one teacher is all it takes. I was lucky because I came to school after the strap, so I was never hit by my teachers or parents. (Living in Sweden sorted that out from the starting blocks.) I remember vividly one of my teachers throwing my homework book at the wall in rage at my illegible handwriting. Or another teacher calling me obnoxious because I asked too many questions.

But my 6th-grade teacher changed my world around from feeling like an obnoxious alien to someone smart - in my own way. Mr Spedding was a part of the Harvard Graduate School of Education Project Zero Research Program, whose mission is to explore and support human potential, such as learning, thinking, ethics, intelligence and creativity. At the time, I hadn't been formally diagnosed with anything apart from being a general nuisance. I had hearing tests that came out normal despite never being able to recall verbal instructions, and the majority of teachers just thought I was a cheeky so-and-so because as soon as they would finish explaining an activity, my hand would shoot up, I would ask them to explain it again, and I'd be told I should listen better. Most of the teachers thought I was just trying to wind them up, perhaps I did enjoy stirring the pot slightly, but in all honesty, words just floated out my ears. I would understand the words the teachers were saying but strung together as verbal instructions, they just floated right out my head.

But this teacher, Mr Spedding, brought our classroom to life to the point that far too many years have passed, and I still remember details of our lessons almost 30 years on. We created civilisations, buried artefacts did big archeological digs. We did maths outside, we acted out English class, wrote screenplays and the biggest thing I remember was Howard Gardeners' theory of multiple intelligences. It was 1996, I was 11 years old, and his classroom and lessons are forever rooted in my mind and shaped me into who I am. I can see my little mobile hanging overhead with my planets of intelligence, reminding me that I am smart, even if areas of academia didn't come naturally. With Mr Spedding at the helm of my education, I felt invincible.

Even after I was diagnosed, I never wore the label of dyslexia or ADHD because I felt ashamed. I felt lesser than. In fact, my father always refuted the idea of my having a learning disability. I think, in his eyes, I was nothing less than perfect. (So are my kids to me today.)

Perfectly imperfect - we all are. I don't feel as though I am a person with a learning disability. I am perfectly capable and smart in my own way, maybe not in the standardised testing kind of way, or someone who can spell without using autocorrect, but in my classroom, Mr Spedding empowered me enough to know that I was, and still am, smart.

So as I matured and researched more into psychology, sociology, and educational pedagogy, I began noticing the term 'neurodiverse'. Literary agents, and publishing houses, were calling out neurodiverse authors. My dyslexia suddenly wasn't something that I needed to hide behind. It was part of my identity and my story, my lens on life.

My goal with this guidebook is for each and every reader to understand and explore how they are smart and understand some of the unique challenges and strengths that other neurodivergent people experience. Perhaps you will understand more about yourself, a family member, a classmate, or a work colleague.

I hope my wild and wacky brain is able to offer you visuals for an open-ended discussion about what it means to be smart and what it can mean to be neurodivergent.

No matter what our differences are called, we all have individual strengths and challenges, things we are smart at, and things we struggle with.

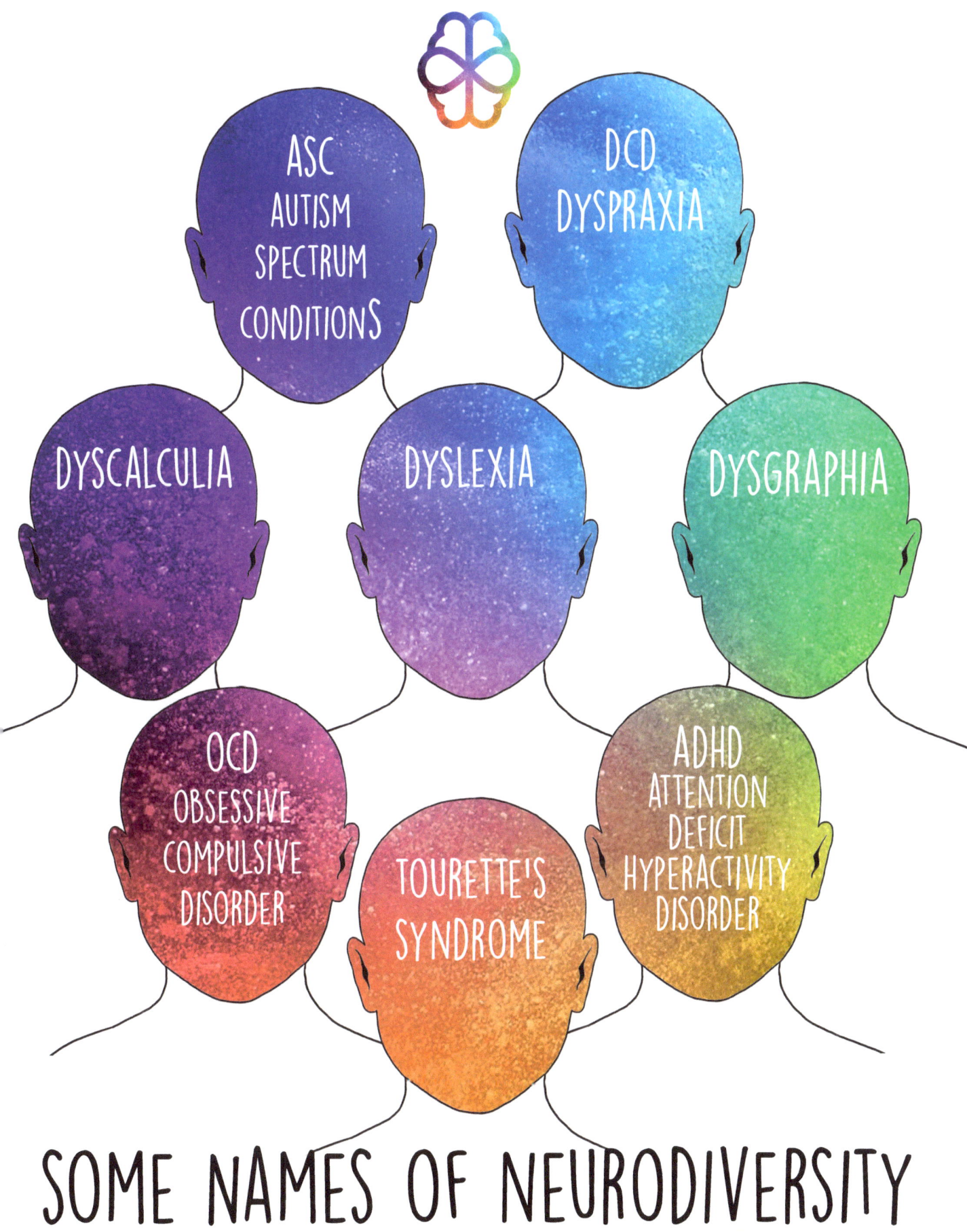

AUTISM SPECTRUM DISORDER

People with autism can have difficulty following non-specific instructions. Autism affects how a person perceives the world, interacts and socialises with others. It can be challenging for people with autism to interpret social cues. People with autism can be sensitive to noise, smells, touch, and lights.

People with autism can be excellent at finding patterns, detail-focused, highly logical and great at absorbing and remembering facts. They are also known for their honesty.

Do you know anyone with autism?

ADHD
ATTENTION DEFICIT HYPERACTIVITY DISORDER

People with ADHD struggle with concentration, and organisation. ADHD affects a persons abilty to focus.

People with ADHD are often very passionate and enthusiastic. They have strong visual skills and an amazing ability to hyper-focus.

*Hyper-focus is a highly focused attention state that can last for a long time and the world outside fades into the background.

Do you know anyone with ADHD?

ADHD Strengths & Challenges

- DIFFICULTY CONCENTRATING
- ALERTNESS AND ABILITY TO HYPER-FOCUS
- STRONG VISUAL SKILLS
- TAKING ON TOO MUCH
- DIFFICULTY WITH PEOPLE (MAY APPEAR RUDE)
- PASSION AND ENTHUSIASM
- PROBLEM SOLVING ABILITIES
- LACKING ATTENTION TO DETAIL

DYSCALCULIA

People with **dys**calculia **str**uggle with **num**bers and **mat**hematic **con**cepts. **Th**ey **ma**y struggle with finances, time **man**agement **an**d **som**etimes **dir**ections.

People with **dys**calculia **are oft**en **ver**y **go**od at **str**ategic **thi**nking **an**d **pro**blem-**sol**ving. **Th**ey **are oft**en **hig**hly **cre**ative **and int**uitive.

Do you know anyone with dyscalculia?

DYSLEXIA

People with dyslexia have difficulty processing language, which can cause reading, writing and spelling challenges.

Dyslexia can also cause challenges with organisation, remembering sounds and putting order into detail.

People with dyslexia are highly creative, great problem solvers, and they have strong visual skills.

About 35% of entrepreneurs have dyslexia.

Do you know anyone with dyslexia?

DYSLEXIA

Strengths & Challenges

- STRONG COMMUNICATION SKILLS
- DIFFICULTY READING AND WRITING
- DIFFICULTY REMEMBERING SOUND
- STRONG 3D VISUAL SKILLS
- GREAT LONG TERM MEMORY
- DIFFICULTY PROCESSING SOUND
- GREAT AT PROBLEM SOLVING
- DIFFICULTY PUTTING DETAIL IN ORDER

DYSPRAXIA
DEVELOPMENTAL COORDINATION DISORDER

People **with dys**praxia **are som**etimes **mis**perceived **as bei**ng **clu**msy **bec**ause **dys**praxia **aff**ects **phy**sical **coo**rdination.

Dyspraxia **can aff**ect fine **mo**tor **ski**lls like **han**dwriting or **the abi**lity to tie **the**ir **sho**elaces. **Dys**praxia **can al**so **aff**ect **gro**ss **mo**tor **ski**lls, like **cat**ching a **ba**ll or **rid**ing a **bi**cycle.

People **with dys**praxia **oft**en **have** a **ve**ry **cre**ative **ima**gination, **are stro**ng **com**municators, **go**od at **acti**ve **lis**tening **and** are **ve**ry **det**ermined.

Do you know anyone with dyspraxia?

DYSPRAXIA
Strengths & Challenges

- TIME MANAGEMENT AND ORGANISATION
- GOOD AT ACTIVE LISTENING AND EMPATHETIC
- A CREATIVE IMAGINATION
- PROBLEMS WITH MOVEMENT AND COORDINATION
- DIFFICULTY FOLLOWING SEQUENCES
- DETERMINATION
- VERBAL COMMUNICATION SKILLS
- DIFFICULTY LEARNING NEW PROCESSES

TOURETTE SYNDROME

People with tourette syndrome have "tics," **which are sudden, uncontrolled, repetitive muscle movements or sounds.**

Different situations may trigger a "tic" **but often stressful situations highlight the tics and make them longer lasting.**

People with Tourette Syndrome are often very creative, have a lot of empathy and are great communicators.

Do you know anyone with tourette syndrome?

OCD OBSESSIVE COMPULSIVE DISORDER

People with OCD can struggle with anxiety and are excessively concerned about illness or injury. Their need to feel in control can lead to repetitive behaviours such as handwashing, arranging objects in a specific way, and repeatedly checking things such as locks, switches or doors.

People with OCD are also very good at time management, have excellent attention to detail, are good delegators and are often highly empathetic and creative.

Do you know anyone with OCD?

OCD. Obsessive Compulsive Disorder
Strengths & Challenges

- Great attention to detail
- Excessive concern about illness or injury
- Good at meeting deadlines
- Need to feel in control
- Over cautious
- Manage time well
- Empathetic and creative
- Anxiety

**There is no right way to think or learn.
Intelligence looks different to everyone.
Challenges are different to everyone.**

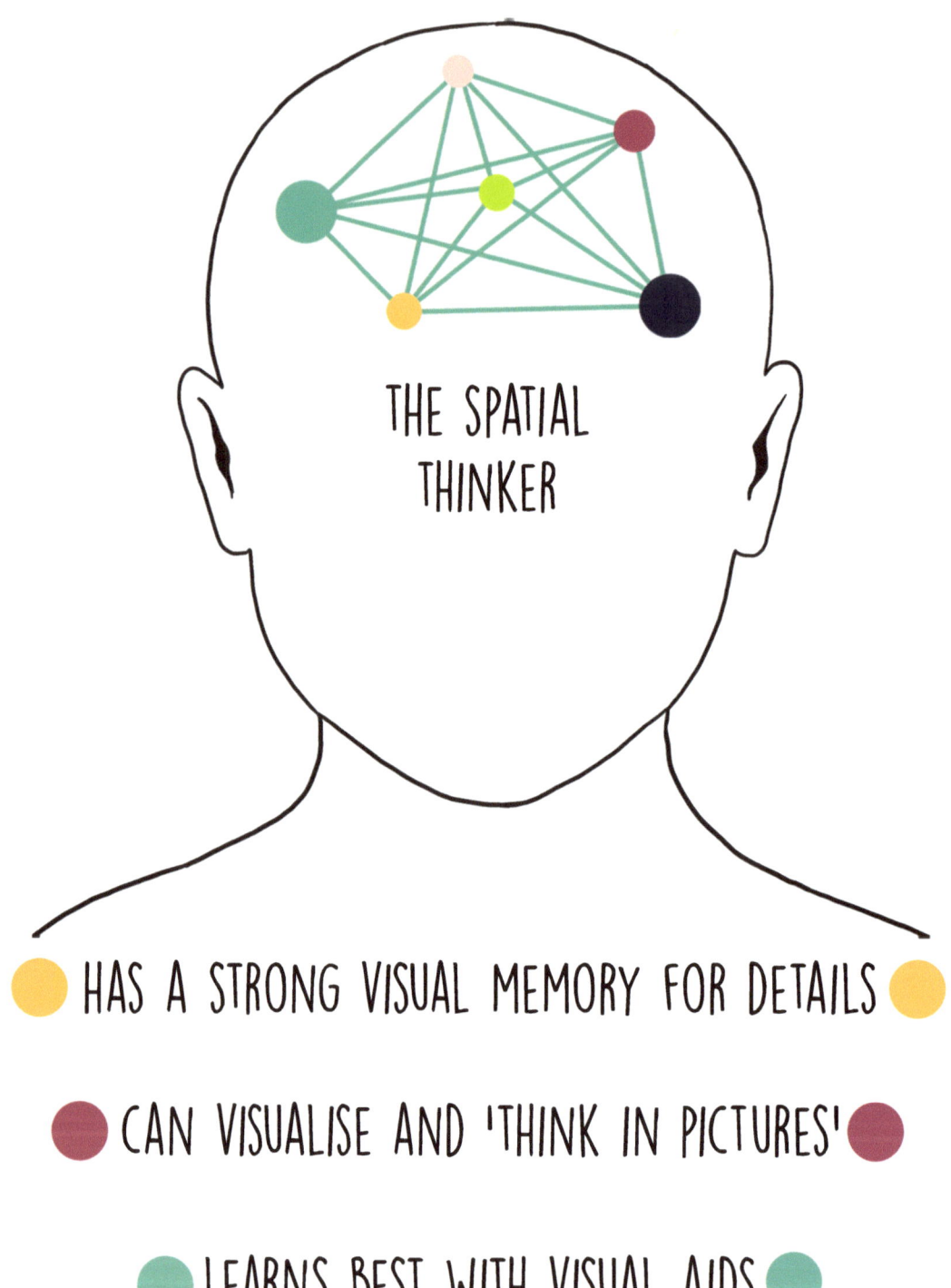

THE SPATIAL THINKER

- HAS A STRONG VISUAL MEMORY FOR DETAILS
- CAN VISUALISE AND 'THINK IN PICTURES'
- LEARNS BEST WITH VISUAL AIDS
- HAS A STRONG EYE FOR DESIGN AND SPATIAL JUDGEMENT

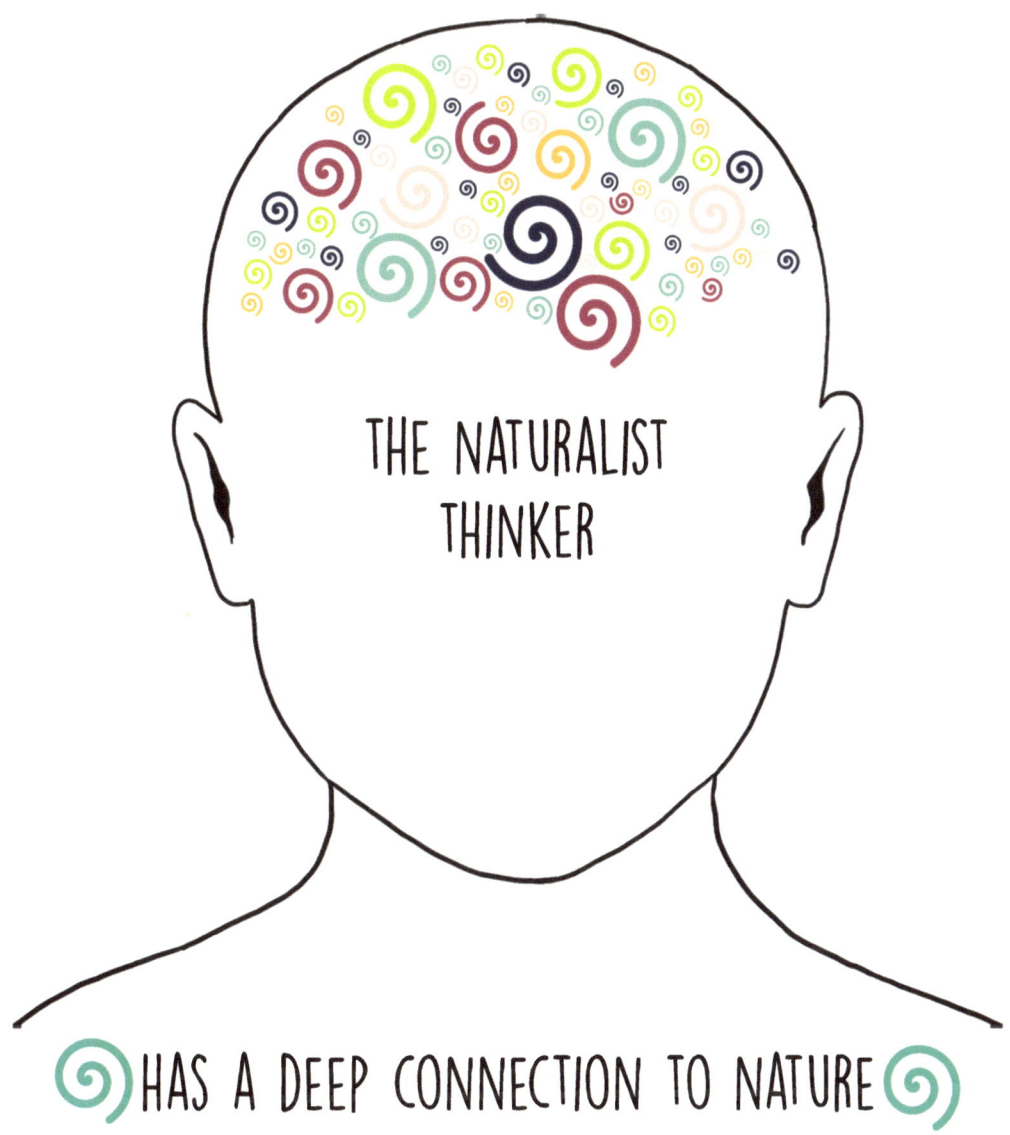

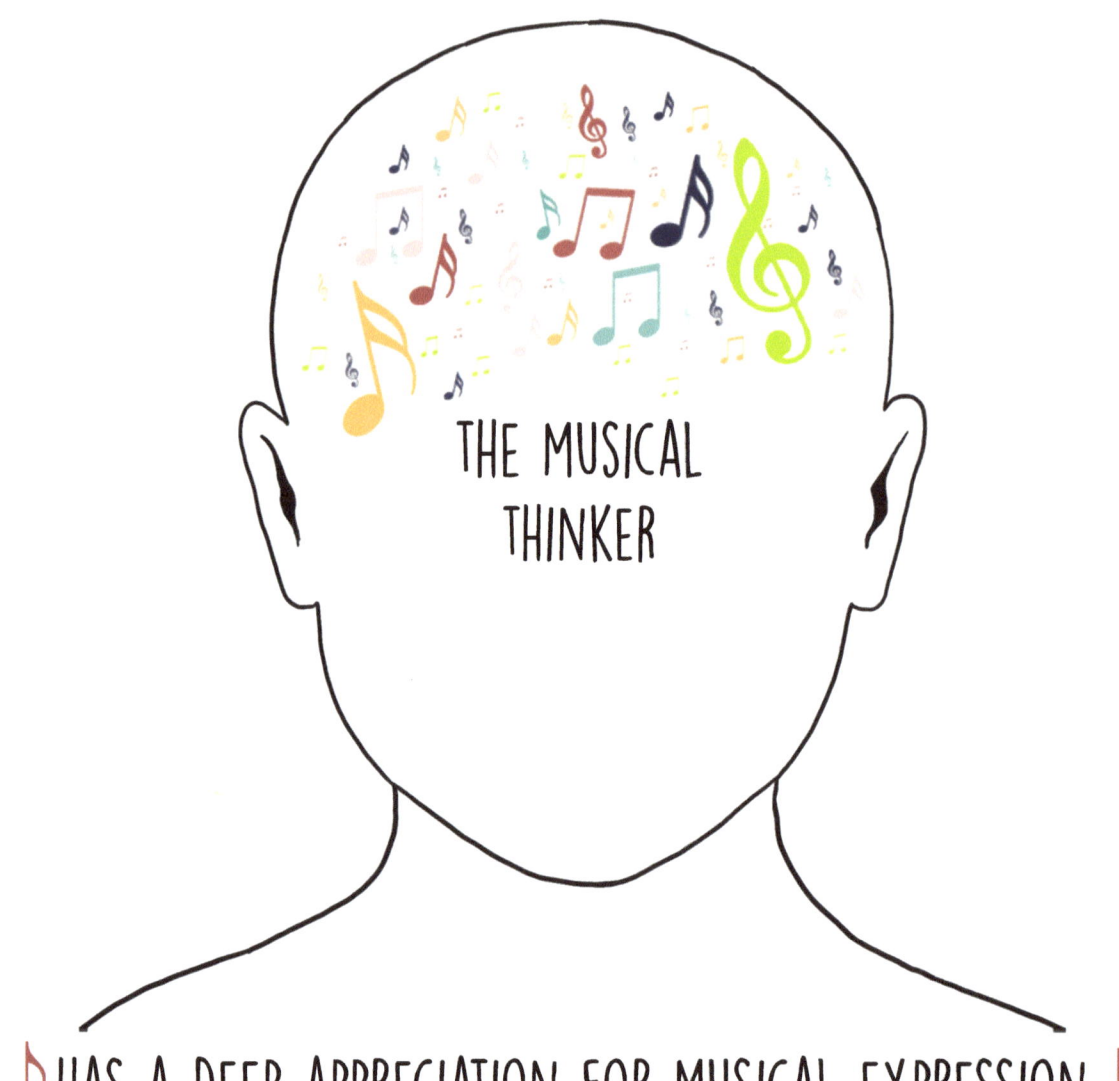

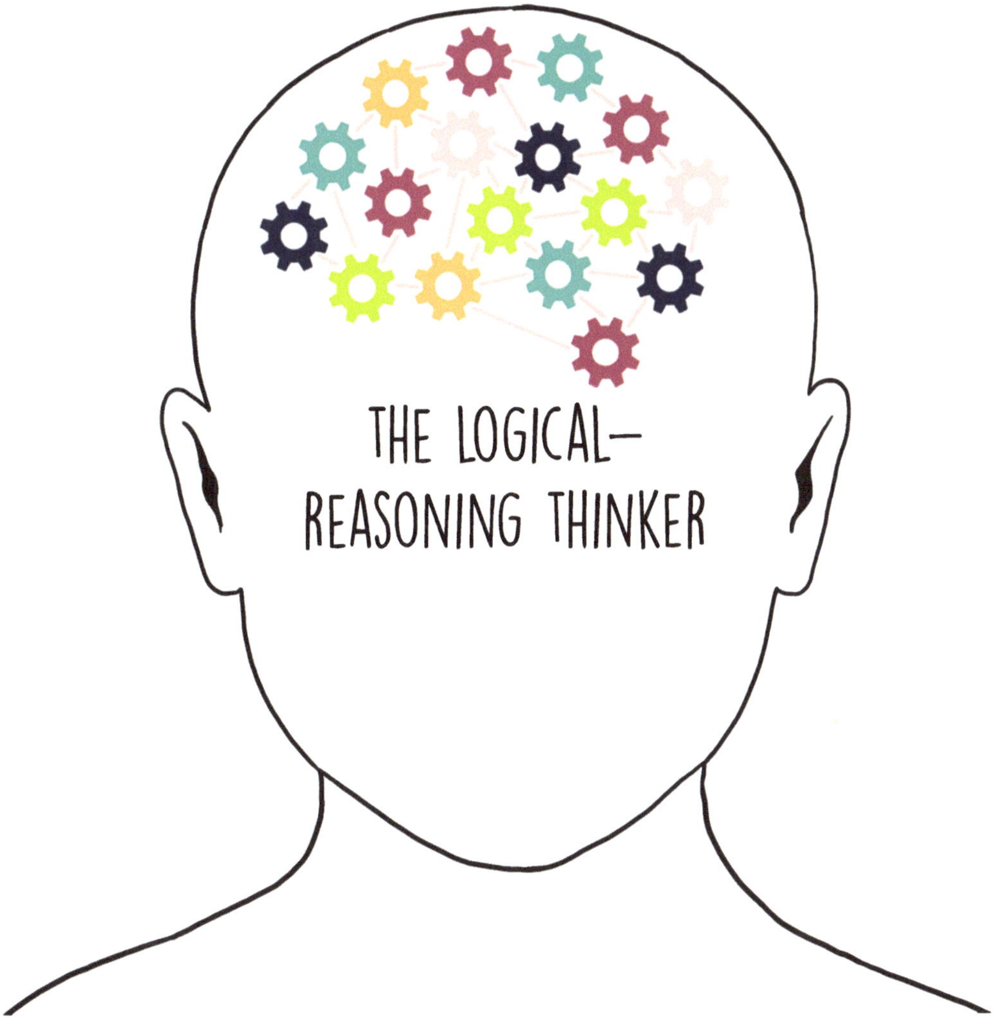

THE LOGICAL—REASONING THINKER

- IS EVIDENCE AND FACT FOCUSED
- IS SKILLED AT FINDING PATTERNS
- HAS A STRONG SCIENTIFIC AND MATHEMATICAL MIND
- IS GOOD AT MAKING HYPOTHESES AND PROVING THEM

THE INTERPERSONAL THINKER

★ IS A POWERFUL COMMUNICATOR ★

★ IS GREAT AT LEADING TEAMS AND GROUPS OF PEOPLE ★

★ LEARNS BEST WITH OTHER PEOPLE, TALKING THROUGH IDEAS ★

★ UNDERSTANDS OTHER PEOPLE AND THEIR MOTIVATIONS ★

THE INTRAPERSONAL THINKER

- UNDERSTAND THEIR FEELINGS AND THOUGHTS
- ENJOY SELF-REFLECTION AND ARE HIGHLY SELF-AWARE
- LEARN BEST ON THEIR OWN
- ARE GOAL ORIENTATED AND ENJOY PERSONAL GROWTH

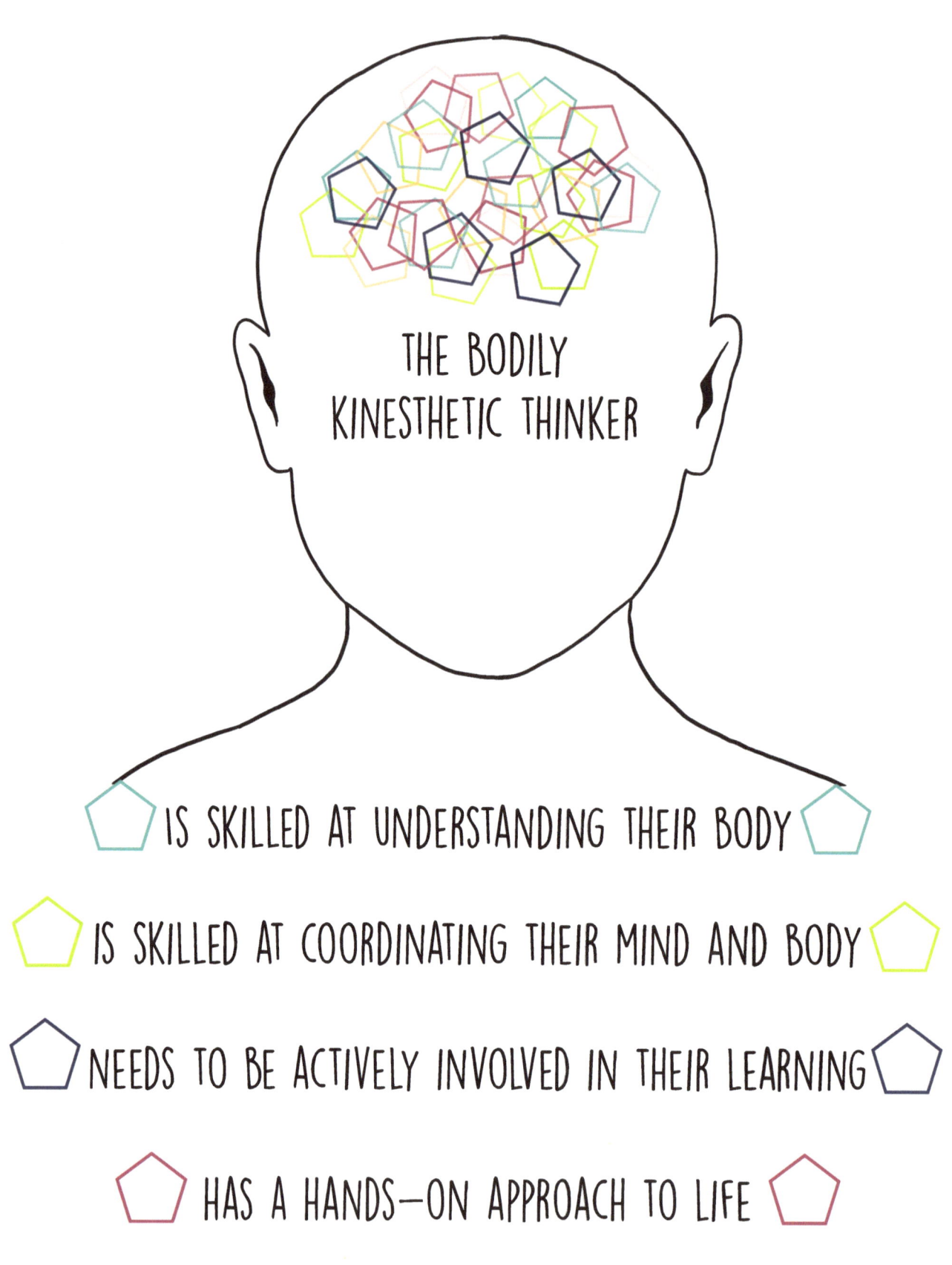

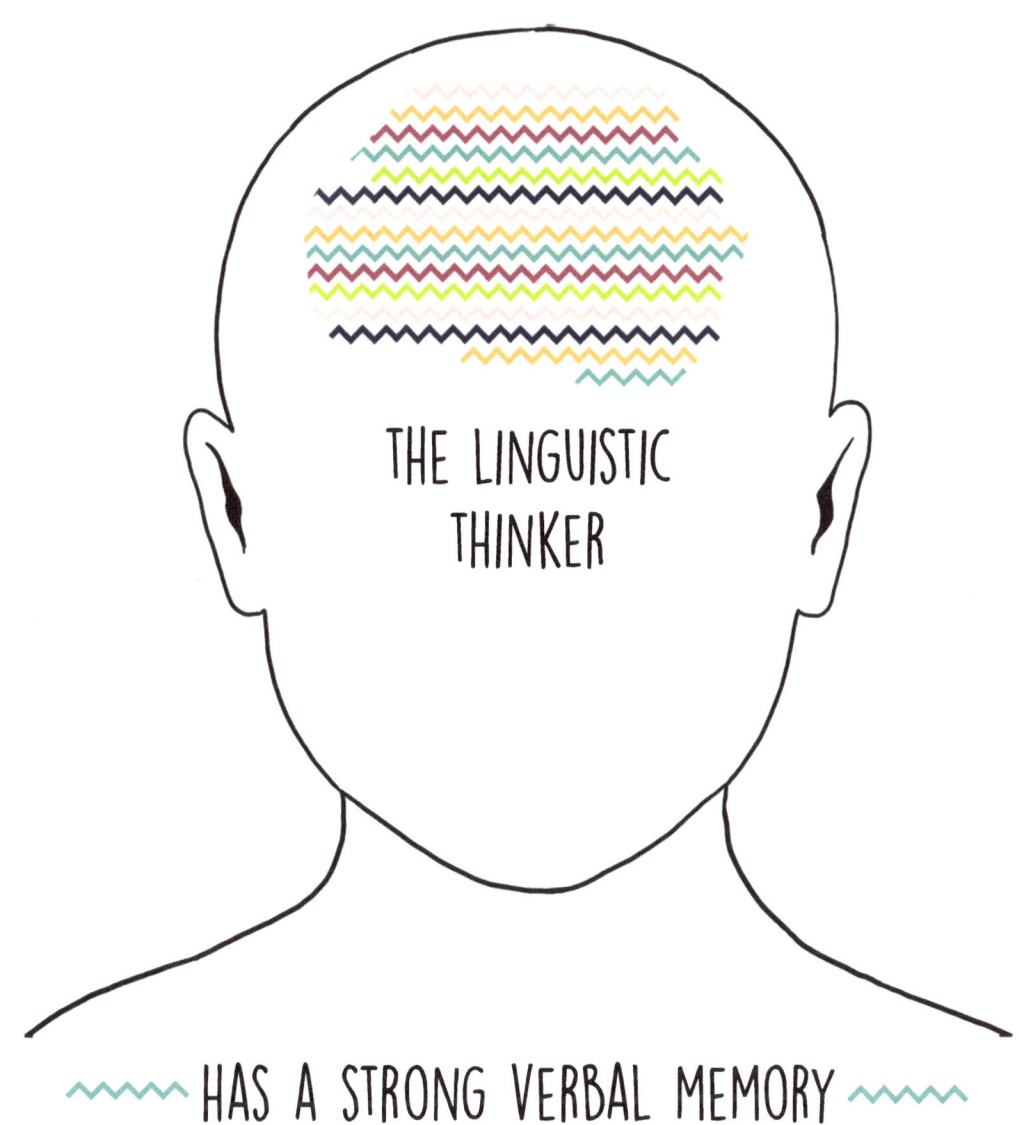

THE LINGUISTIC THINKER

~~~ HAS A STRONG VERBAL MEMORY ~~~

~~~ IS GREAT AT USING WORDS TO EXPRESS THEMSELVES ~~~

~~~ LEARNS BEST WITH SPOKEN OR WRITTEN MATERIAL ~~~

~~~ UNDERSTANDS LANGUAGE AND THINKS LOGICALLY ~~~

Think about your intelligence as planets floating around you. The bigger planets are the things you are naturally better at, your strengths. The smaller planets are things you find challenging or haven't figured out yet.

EXAMPLE.

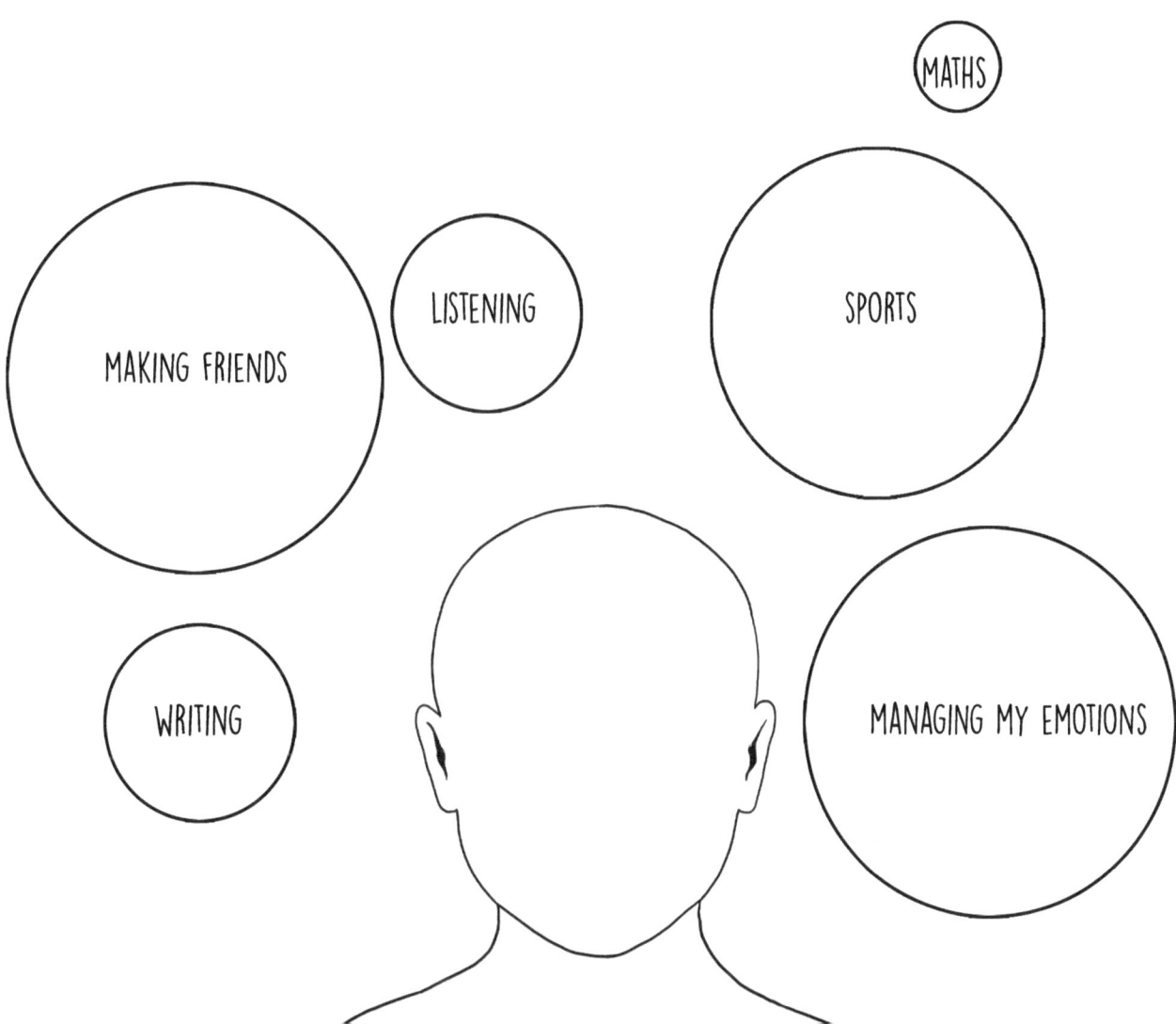

HOW AM I SMART?

HOW DO I KNOW?

WHAT CONSTELLATION OF INTELLIGENCES ARE MANIFEST IN WHEN YOU ARE:

RIDING A BIKE?

WALKING DOWN THE SIDEWALK?

SPENDING THE DAY WITH YOUR FAMILY AT THE BEACH?

CLEANING YOUR ROOM?

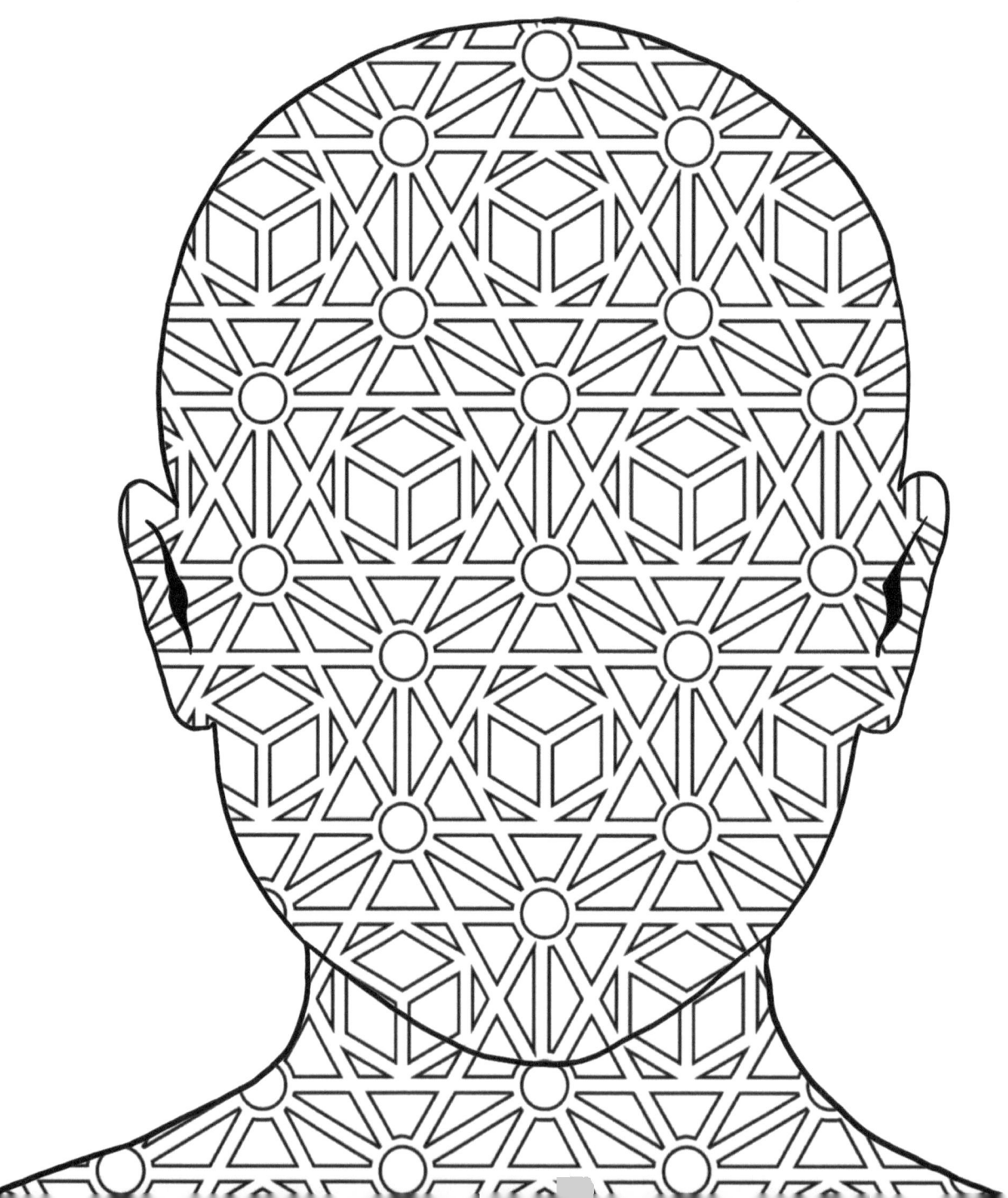

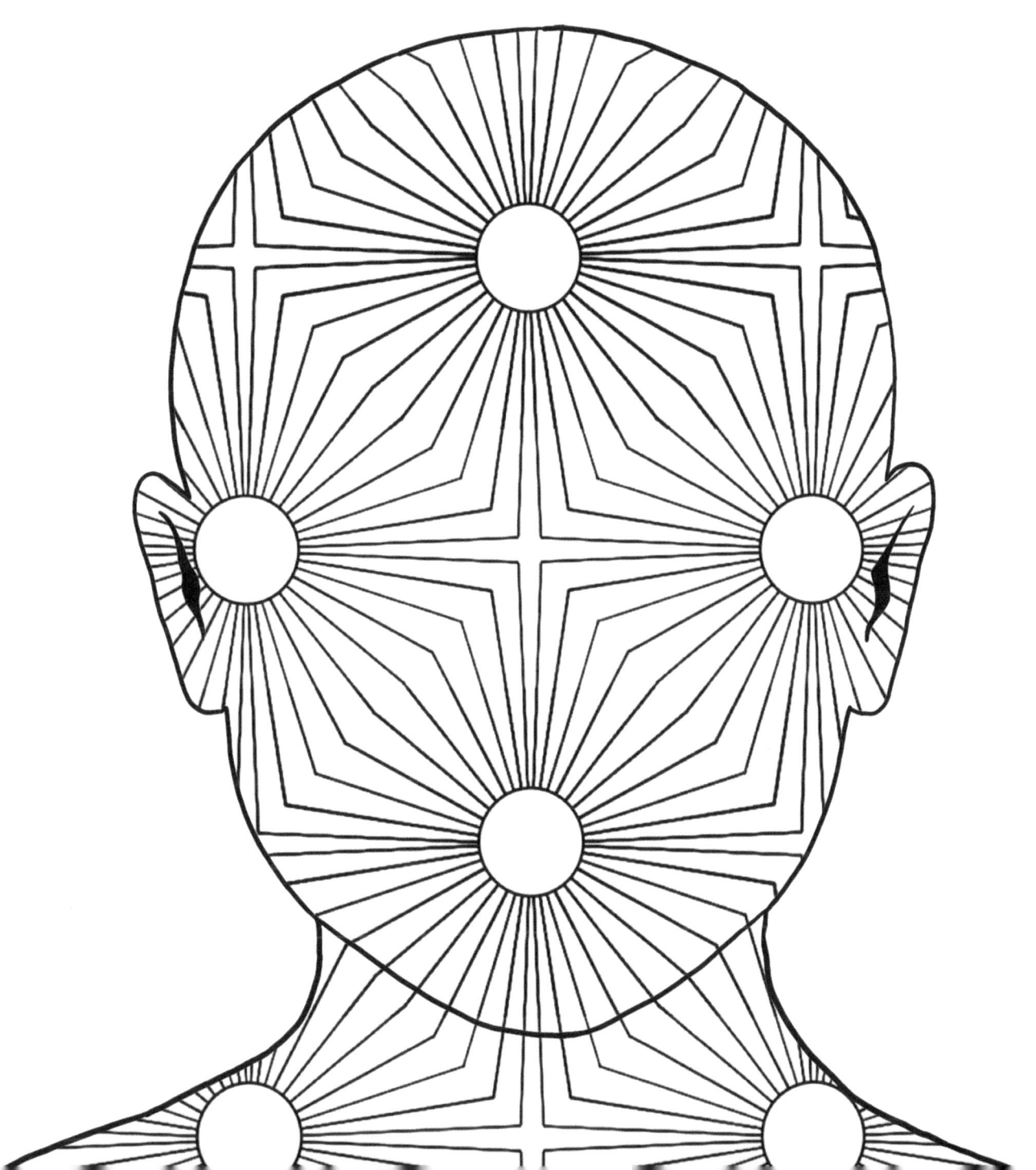

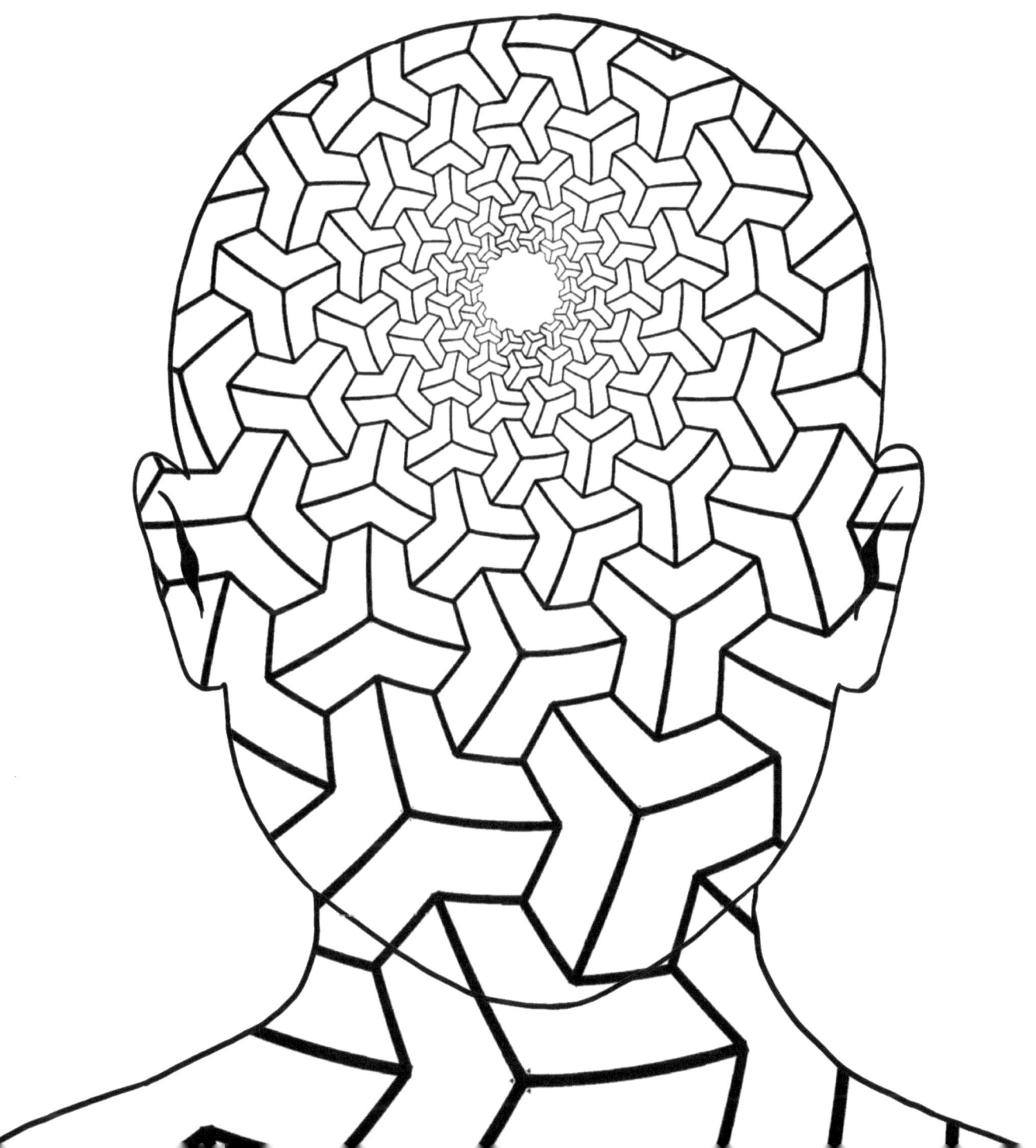

SOURCES

Lexxic The Leading Neurodiversity Experts in the UK **https://lexxic.com/**

MI Oasis, Howard Gardner's official authoritative site of Multiple Intelligences: **https://www.multipleintelligencesoasis.org/**

Neurodiversity Celebration Week **https://www.neurodiversityweek.com/**

Project Zero: **https://pz.harvard.edu**

Gardener, Howard (1983) Frames of Mind, The Theory of Multiple Intelligences. New York, Basic Books.

Singer, Judy (2017) NeuroDiversity The Birth of an Idea. Sydney, Amazon

Silberman, Steve (2015) Neurotribes: The legacy of autism and the future of neurodiversity. New York, Avery.

A NOTE ON LANGUAGE

The language of neurodiversity has been evolving for some time, but I'm conscious that the term itself is still in flux. I have been plagued with whether or not to capitalise the term neurodiversity as the language itself was not set by a clinical framework but a term that has emerged from within the community to describe their own identity and belonging.

Please know I've done my best to represent an emerging framework, and I will continue to study and grow alongside this movement as the language becomes more crystallised from within.

ABOUT HEATHER JESSE RAY

Heather Ray is an author/illustrator and wellbeing program designer. Heather studied Applied Theatre and Education at the Royal Central School of Speech and Drama, where her taste for education took off. She later qualified as a Body Control Pilates Instructor, moved to Hong Kong to study Chinese Kung Fu, and co-founded a Health and Wellbeing Club in the City Centre in 2008. In 2013, Heather moved to Cyprus to study psychotherapy and meditation with a spiritual group called the Researchers of Truth. There, her work became more focused on counselling, healing, and meditation. In 2017, Heather moved to Australia, where she now calls home, and founded My Wellbeing School. Heather's flare for creativity, design, wealth of wellbeing expertise, and relatable character make her programs engaging and irresistible to families, schools, and therapists alike.

MORE BOOKS BY H. J. RAY

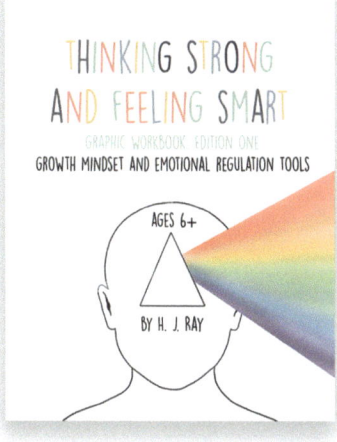

www.ingramcontent.com/pod-product-compliance
Lightning Source LLC
Chambersburg PA
CBHW041430010526
44107CB00046B/1565